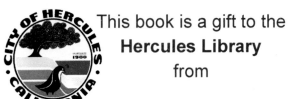

Langston Hughes

CREATIVE EDITIONS

J. PATRICK LEWIS

FREEDOM LIKE SUNLIGHT

PRAISESONGS FOR BLACK AMERICANS

JOHN THOMPSON

For Tom Peterson, with admiration and gratitude. J.P.L.

For my father, Roy Thompson, an artist and avid jazz fan. J.T.

Text copyright © 2000 by J. Patrick Lewis / Illustrations copyright © 2000 by John Thompson
Published in 2003 by Creative Editions, 123 South Broad Street, Mankato, MN 56001 USA
Creative Editions is an imprint of The Creative Company. Designed by Rita Marshall
Library of Congress Cataloging-in-Publication Data: Lewis, J. Patrick. Freedom like sunlight:
praisesongs for Black Americans / by J. Patrick Lewis; illustrated by John Thompson.
Summary: Presents poems and brief biographical notes about such well-known African-Americans
as Arthur Ashe, Harriet Tubman, Sojourner Truth, Martin Luther King Jr., "Satchel" Paige,
Rosa Parks, Jesse Owens, Marian Anderson, Malcolm X, Wilma Rudolph, and Billie Holiday.
ISBN 1-56846-163-1 I. Afro-Americans—Biography—Juvenile poetry.
2. Afro-Americans—History—Juvenile poetry. 3. Children's poetry, American.
[I. Afro-Americans—Poetry. 2. American poetry.] I. Title.
PS3562.E9465F74   2000   811'.54—dc21   98-50909
10 9 8 7 6

Contents

ARTHUR ASHE

THE MAN WHO BECAME A WORD

I

Blue was the land and black the native son,

Who came one day and quietly took the prize.

He served into the wind at Wimbledon,

Then, like a giant, autographed the skies.

II

The game went on and life went on, but he

Stood Fortitude and Terror face to face,

And for the first time ever we would see

A man become a word. The word was Grace.

HARRIET TUBMAN

ABOLITIONIST AND UNDERGROUND RAILROAD CONDUCTOR   1820-1913

HARRIET TUBMAN SPEAKS

I packed some corn bread
And salt herring.
I packed my favorite patchwork quilt.
The shabby rags
That I was wearing
Came from the House that Evil built.

North woods were strange
To me, a stranger,
When Lady Freedom took my hand.
She said, "Brown girl,
Brown girl, the danger
Still hunts beyond the Promised Land."

But nineteen times
I turned the handle
For folks beat down Indignity Lane.
Three hundred slaves,
Who took the candle
And fled the whip and the bamboo cane,

Said Lady Freedom's
Tea was sweeter
Than all the honey in a shut-up hive.
Said they were glad
At last to meet her,
Said nothing's as sweet as being alive.

SOJOURNER TRUTH

AMERICAN EVANGELIST AND REFORMER   1797?-1883

AIN'T I A WOMAN?

I was Isabella born,

Children, hear my cry,

And I was child to scalding scorn,

Children, hear my cry.

Chorus

Hold on, Jesus, ain't I a woman born?

Tell the children, let them hear my cry.

Mister Dumont bought me cheap,

Children, hear my cry,

A hundred dollars and a flock of sheep,

Children, hear my cry.

Chorus . . .

Well, Mister Dumont tracked me down,

Children, hear my cry,

He swore he'd whip me through the town,

Children, hear my cry.

Chorus . . .

They took my child away from me,

Children, hear my cry.

Said Peter disappeared at sea,

Children, hear my cry.

Chorus . . .

I go on preaching freedom's fire,

Children, hear my cry.

It ain't for sale and it ain't for hire,

Children, hear my cry.

Chorus . . .

To be sung to "Go Down, Moses"

LOUIS "SATCHMO" ARMSTRONG

TRUMPETER, SINGER, COMPOSER, BANDLEADER   1900-1971

NICKEL-A-BUCKET TUNE

How that pie man played the bugle
Down in Looziana where I was born.
Waffle man rang a big triangle,
Junkman leaned on a long tin horn.
Always something nice in New Orleans.

Pushed a coal cart, nickel-a-bucket,
Nickel-a-bucket's what I got paid.
Junkman's helper! Bought my supper
Leading this poor man's parade.

First King Oliver, then Kid Ory
Blew some horns that blew my mind.
Listen, kid, while I tell my story,
Left that nickel-a-bucket behind.

Jammed in dives and honky-tonks,
And most gigs in between.
London, Paris, Carnegie Hall,
Then I blew down the Delta Queen.

Sang my songs like sand on gravel,
Blew my horn and pretty soon,
No more nickel-a, nickel-a, nickel-a,
No more nickel-a-bucket tunes.
Always something nice in New Orleans.

MARTIN LUTHER KING, JR.

CIVIL RIGHTS LEADER   1929-1968

HOW LONG? NOT LONG, BECAUSE NO LIE CAN LIVE FOREVER

For having told
    The truth, I am
Alone and cold
    In Birmingham.

I speak to them,
    They spit at me
Because it's Mem-
    phis, Tennessee.

The evening news
    From Selma's jail
Cannot excuse
    This brute betrayal.

Though I am tired,
    I've just begun.
But someone's fired
    The fateful gun.

I hear the shot,
    I feel the pain. . . .
Who bravely fought
    Must fight again.

LEROY "SATCHEL" PAIGE

BASEBALL PITCHER   1906-1982

FATHER TIME IS COMING

Out of a windmill windup,
the whipcord arm grooves a dartball
on a string past the hopeful, waiting
at the plate for a miracle.

It might have been the bee ball,
　　　the looper,
　　　　　　the drooper,
　　　　　　　　　the jump ball,
　　　　　　　　　　　　the wobbly ball,
　　　the two-hump blooper,
　　　　　　the bat dodger,
　　　　　　　　　the famous hesi-
　　　　　　tation pitch,
　　　or the radioball "You hears it,
　　　　　　but you never sees it."

Joe DiMaggio couldn't hit him.
And said so.
Babe Ruth never faced him.
Lucky Bambino.
"I'm Satchel," he said,
"I do as I do."

ROSA PARKS

CIVIL RIGHTS ACTIVIST   1913-

THE MANY AND THE FEW

It was an Alabama day
For both the Many and the Few.
There wasn't really much to do;
No one had very much to say

Until a bus, the 4:15,
Drove by. But no one chanced to see
It stop to pick up history.
The doors closed slowly on a scene:

The quiet seamstress paid her fare
And took the one seat she could find,
And, as it happened, just behind
The Many People sitting there.

The Many People paid no mind
Until the driver, J. P. Blake,
Told the Few of *them* to take
The deeper seats. But she declined.

Blake stopped the bus and called police;
And Many a fire was set that night,
And Many a head turned ghostly white
Because she dared disturb the peace.

To celebrate the ride that marks
The debt the Many owe the Few,
That day of freedom grew into
The Century of Rosa Parks.

LANGSTON HUGHES

POET 1902-1967

BECAUSE MY MOUTH IS WIDE WITH LAUGHTER

Someone said they saw you in Paris
Out on the boulevard strolling along,
And you were shaking down autumn
     With your small song.

Someone said they saw you in Africa.
Winter burned on the dust-green plains.
You and the elders were measuring tears
     Like little rains.

Someone said they saw you in Harlem
As spring crocused up Lenox Avenue,
Laughing with Countee Cullen the way
     You used to do.

Someone said they saw you, Langston,
Spiriting summer. What was it they heard?
Poems that endlessly echoed . . .
     A dream deferred.

JESSE OWENS

I Decided...To Stay Up in the Air Forever

In 1936 Adolf Hitler sat

in his new Olympic Stadium,

eating a Bratwurst and sweating destiny.

110,000 fans waited for the Games

to begin, then something happened

he could not bear to watch.

Onto the track stepped the world's

fastest human, who was not Aryan.

Not white.

Not worthy.

Not welcome.

The Fuhrer looked away without seeing

the man jump over Germany,

jump beyond hope and gravity,

beyond the dreams of ordinary people,

farther than any other human would jump

for the next twenty-four years.

MARIAN ANDERSON

SINGER   1902–1993

BABY CONTRALTO

She brushed

Her voice

    Across the air

In colors

Not seen

    Anywhere.

In colors

Beautiful

    And strong,

She brushed

The air . . .

    And painted song.

MALCOLM X

BLACK RIGHTS ACTIVIST   1925-1965

MY PEOPLE

My brothers weather winters of defeat
And go without a coat or crust of bread;

My sisters sweat in suffocating heat
Of human hate and poverty and dread.

Our mothers should not bear the frost of pain
That creeps in windows all across this land;

Our fathers know the only hope of gain
Comes to those who turn and stop—and stand.

My people soaked up freedom like sunlight,
Living under the bullwhip and the gun.

Today the day holds on against the night,
Because the fight for justice has begun.

WILMA RUDOLPH

TRACK STAR, OLYMPIC GOLD MEDALIST 1940-1994
THE BLACK GAZELLE

In Rome, she was the Black Gazelle.

In Paris, France, Black Pearl.

But who would think

That anything could come

Of such a girl?

At five, she had a crooked leg,

She wore a steel brace.

And who would think

That anyone like her

Could win a race?

But you can hear the legend now

Where stranger tales are told:

At twenty,

She delighted Rome,

Three times Olympic gold.

And there are those who saw her run

Who still remember well:

In Paris, France,

She was Black Pearl,

In Rome, the Black Gazelle.

BILLIE HOLIDAY

SINGER   1915-1959

LADY DAY

Lady could pour you a song,
Coffee and a little cream.
Stir it the whole night long
Into a brown-sugar dream.

Lady could wrap you a note
Up in a velvet night—
Sometimes Manhattan satin,
Always Harlem delight.

Lady Day could sing it
Like nobody ever has
At the Shim Sham Club, Hot Cha Cha,
Joints that swung on jazz.

Her bittersweet songs told Heartbreak,
Meet your sister Pain,
But Lady melted yesterdays
Into beautiful rain.

Rosa Parks

The Man Who Became a Word: Arthur Ashe emerged from his hometown courts in Richmond, Virginia, to become the first black male to gain prominence in world tennis. Noted for his style and grace, as well as an outstanding topspin and backhand, he won the 1968 U.S. Open, the 1970 Australian Open, the 1975 Wimbledon title, and was later named captain of the U.S. Davis Cup Team. In 1992 he announced that he had acquired AIDS from a blood transfusion during a heart operation years earlier. In the last year of his life, he continued to speak out on civil rights and AIDS issues. (p. 6)

Harriet Tubman Speaks: One of the most successful "conductors" on the Underground Railroad, Harriet Tubman is known as the "Moses of her People." A slave herself, she led 300 slaves to freedom, even when it took a loaded revolver to encourage the timid to follow her. Eventually a reward of $40,000 was posted for her capture. In the Civil War, she became a nurse, laundress, and spy for the Union Army in South Carolina. Despite receiving many honors and tributes, including a medal from Queen Victoria, she lived out her long life in poverty in Auburn, New York, not receiving a pension until thirty years after the Civil War. (p. 8)

"Ain't I a Woman?": A gifted speaker, although illiterate, an abolitionist and a freed slave, Sojourner Truth, born Isabella Baumfree, took her new name because she was convinced she heard heavenly voices. Believing that as a black woman she was part of a great drama of robbery and wrong, this fiery preacher traveled throughout the North, speaking out on subjects ranging from abolition to temperance, prison reform, and women's suffrage. (p. 10)

Nickel-a-Bucket Tune: In New Orleans, on New Year's Day 1913, Louis "Satchmo" Armstrong picked up a pistol and fired it. He was subsequently arrested and sent to reform school. It was at the Waif's Home that he first learned to play the bugle. He formed a band when he was 14—the first rung on the ladder of his many musical successes. He had a one-of-a-kind, zest-for-life personality that shined through his trumpet-playing and his rich, gravelly voice. From 1923 to 1970, he cut more than 1,500 records. He was greeted by royalty, honored by U.S. presidents and foreign heads of state. Wherever he went—in America or around the world—he captivated audiences. (p. 12)

"How Long? Not Long, Because No Lie Can Live Forever": This line is taken from Martin Luther King Jr.'s "Our God Is Marching On!" speech, given at the conclusion of the Selma-to-Montgomery March, on March 25, 1965. The son of a Southern Baptist pastor, Dr. King became one of the foremost civic leaders of his or any other time. His philosophy of nonviolent resistance led to his many arrests in the 1950s and 1960s. He was awarded the Nobel Peace Prize in 1964. On April 4, 1968, he was shot and killed by an assassin's bullet on the balcony of the motel where he was staying. (p. 14)

"Father Time Is Coming": A quote from the quotable Casey Stengel, manager of the New York Yankees, who warned his players to score runs early because the St. Louis Browns would soon be sending in the ageless Leroy "Satchel" Paige, known as "Father Time," to relieve the starting pitcher. Satchel became a legend—both for his wit and his pitching—while barnstorming in the Negro baseball leagues before he was finally accepted into the major leagues. He is credited with more than 50 no-hitters. In 1948, at the age of 42, he joined the Cleveland Indians and pitched for another six seasons. He was the first player from the Negro leagues to be inducted into the Baseball Hall of Fame. (p. 18)

The Many and the Few: The Civil Rights Movement was born on December 1, 1955, when Rosa Parks, a part-time seamstress in Montgomery, Alabama, refused to give up her seat to a white man and move to the back of the bus, which was reserved for "Colored People." The Montgomery bus boycott lasted over a year, and by the time it ended, the Supreme Court had ruled segregation on city buses unconstitutional. The boycott also brought to national attention Dr. Martin Luther King Jr. In 1957, Mrs. Parks moved to Detroit, where she remained active in the civil rights movement. (p. 20)

Because My Mouth Is Wide With Laughter: These are the first two lines of "Minstrel Man," a poem by Langston Hughes. From an early age, Hughes led a nomad's life, moving from city to city and country to country, taking numerous jobs, such as a waiter, truck farmer, and seaman. His first book, *The Weary Blues*,

published when he was 24, enabled him to go to college. He was to become a central figure in the Harlem Renaissance. Most of his work, which often uses dialect and jazz rhythms, depicts the life of the urban African American. (p. 22)

"I Decided…To Stay Up in the Air Forever": Jesse Owens' comment before his third and final long-jump—a world-record 26 feet, 5.25 inches—in the 1936 Olympic Games in Berlin. It was there also that Owens astounded fans everywhere by equaling the world mark in the 100-meters, breaking the 200-meter world record, helping the U.S. win the 400-meter relay—and upsetting Hitler's "Aryan theories" of white superiority. (p. 24)

Baby Contralto: Marian Anderson's nickname. The remarkable range of her voice made her a sensation in both opera and Negro spirituals. She was the first black to be named a permanent member of the Metropolitan Opera, and the first black to perform at the White House. But in 1939 the Daughters of the American Revolution would not allow her to perform at Constitution Hall in the nation's capital. Eleanor Roosevelt resigned from the DAR in protest and sponsored Anderson's concert at the Lincoln Memorial. Miss Anderson was named alternate delegate to the United Nations in 1958 and was awarded the President's Medal of Freedom in 1963. (p. 26)

My People: Malcolm X achieved fame and notoriety as a strict segregationist, black supremacist, and an outspoken critic of racist America. After his departure from the Black Muslims over political ideas and a pilgrimage to Mecca in 1964, he converted to Orthodox Islam, and his views mellowed. He now subscribed to the belief that blacks and whites could coexist in peace. In February 1965 he was shot and killed at the Audubon Ballroom in New York City. Though Black Muslims have always been suspected in the murder, the true identity of the killers is still in doubt. (p. 28)

The Black Gazelle: As a young girl, the 20th of 22 children, Wilma Rudolph suffered from polio, scarlet fever, and double pneumonia (twice). Her mother took her to Nashville for weekly heat and water therapy. Wilma's brothers and sisters massaged her crippled leg at least four times each day. At age five, she was fitted for a metal brace, which she wore for the next six years, until her condition improved. She overcame polio to become one of the finest track athletes of her time. Miss Rudolph won many honors, including the Sullivan Award in 1961. (p. 32)

Lady Day: At age 15, Billie Holiday began singing professionally. After performing with many bands, especially those of Benny Goodman, Teddy Wilson, Count Basie, and Artie Shaw, she began a solo career in nightclubs and theaters that made her the supreme modern jazz singer. Her voice was rough and lush, with phrasing all its own, and emotion that brushed the soul. Miss Holiday suffered many personal tragedies, including a drug addiction that she could not overcome, which eventually ended her career and hastened her death at the age of 44. (p. 34)